MISS NILE'S MUMMY LESSONS

Pickle Hill Primary

Mr Day's Knight Lessons
Phil Roxbee Cox

Mr Fossil's Dinosaur Lessons
Valerie Wilding

Miss Galaxy's Space Lessons
Phil Roxbee Cox

Mr Megamouth's Shark Lessons
Michael Cox

Mrs Parrot's Rainforest Lessons
Michael Cox

Miss Scorcher's Desert Lessons
Valerie Wilding

MISS NILE'S MUMMY

LESSONS

Alan MacDonald

illustrated by

Kelly Waldek

■SCHOLASTIC

Scholastic Children's Books,
Commonwealth House, 1–19 New Oxford Street,
London WC1A 1NU, UK

A division of Scholastic Ltd
London ~ New York ~ Toronto ~ Sydney ~ Auckland
Mexico City ~ New Delhi ~ Hong Kong

Published in the UK by Scholastic Ltd, 2003

ISBN 0 439 97819 X

Typeset by M Rules
Printed by Nørhaven Paperbacks A/S, Denmark

2 4 6 8 10 9 7 5 3 1

Contents

Welcome to Pickle Hill Primary!   7

Creepy!   10

Kiss kiss – it's Pharaoh   25

Ye gods!   39

How to make a mummy   56

Let's hold a funeral!   70

Tomb with a view   83

Pet mummies   95

Tomb robbers   106

Raiders of the lost tomb   114

Welcome to Pickle Hill Primary!

Hi, my name is Sammy C and I go to Pickle Hill Primary. On the outside it looks just like any ordinary old school, but don't be fooled... inside it's magic!

Take the teachers. Maybe you think you've got some weird ones at your school. Well, you should meet some of ours! This book is all about Miss Nile and her amazing mummy lessons. Miss Nile's potty about anything to do with ancient Egypt — the creepier the better. She's not scared of anything — even meeting a mummy in the flesh doesn't give her goosebumps!

At Pickle Hill, lessons are never boring cos you never know what might happen next. At any moment, a piece of pyramid might drop through the ceiling or a Pharaoh might thunder through the classroom in his chariot. You might find yourself watching a mummy being made (revolting!). You might even join a gang of tomb robbers...

Join me and the rest of 5B for Miss Nile's mummy lessons — they're dead exciting!

by Sammy C

Teacher's name: **Miss Nile**

Age: **A secret (but we'll find out).**

Appearance: **Tall, dark and jangly.**

Subject: **History.**

Favourite topic: **Mummies! Yikes!**

Quirks, tics or odd behaviour:

Fearless, but can sometimes be forgetful. Dances when she gets excited. Likes to scare her class.

Information supplied by: **Sammy C**

9

Creepy!

We were all busy talking when Miss Nile slammed a box down on her desk.

The whole class jumped about a mile in the air – we hadn't even heard her come in. Miss Nile's always springing up out of nowhere like a jack-in-the-box. You'd think that with all those jangly gold bangles we'd hear her coming. Queenie, the school cat, had slinked in, too, and was sniffing the box.

"Sorry, Queenie," said Miss Nile. "Nothing for you in there!"

"What *is* in there?" my pal Sean asked.

Miss Nile slowly opened the lid. Peter Trimble (or Tremble, as we call him) got ready to run, in case the box was full of spiders. But instead, Miss Nile drew out rolls of thin white material that seemed to go on for ever.

"Can anyone guess what it is?" Miss Nile asked.

Jane Maclane, the class megabrain, shot up her hand. "Bandages!" she said. "We're going to do First Aid."

Miss Nile shook her head. "Not a bad guess. But this is special material called linen. Sammy, why don't you try it for size?"

With that, Miss Nile started to wind the linen round my head! I felt a bit daft, but not as daft as I looked.

My friends all giggled.

"It's a big improvement," laughed Sunny Dev, who's always cracking jokes.

"Vemmy fummy," I mumbled from inside the bandages.

"I know," shouted one of the twins. "He's a mummy!"

"Right!" said Miss Nile. "This week we're going to be looking at my all-time favourite subject – mummies!"

Everyone started talking at once.

Miss Nile had started to tap her feet. When she's excited, she does this little dance and her gold earrings and bangles jangle like crazy. She loves anything ancient and the spookier it is, the better. "So, who knows what a mummy is?" she asked.

"Someone who makes your sandwiches," said Kevin.

Jane "the brain" Maclane corrected him. "A mummy's a dead body that hasn't gone rotten."

"Right, Jane," said Miss Nile. "And, actually, the word 'mummy' has nothing to do with mummies and daddies. It comes from an Arab word, *mummiya*, which means 'bitumen'."

"Bitu who?" asked Sunny.

"It's a sort of black tar," Miss Nile explained. "People first thought the sticky stuff on mummies was bitumen."

"Urgh! Was it really dried blood?" asked Sean.

"No, it was the sticky oils and resins used in mummy-making," said Miss Nile. "We'll hear more about that later. Sammy, did you want to ask a question?"

"Mmm mmm mmm!" I said. Did I mention that Miss Nile can be forgetful? This time, she'd completely forgotten that I was still tied up in bandages!

"I'm so sorry, Sammy," she said, going a little pink. "I thought you were a little quieter than usual."

As she pulled off my bandages, Miss Nile told us more about her favourite subject. "Not all mummies were wrapped in linen," she said. "The first ones were made by accident. For instance, you can get mummies that have been frozen, dried or even pickled."

"You mean like pickled onions?" asked Sunny.

"Exactly like that," said Miss Nile. "What causes a dead body to decay is oxygen."

"Isn't that what we breathe?" asked Sunny.

"It is," said Miss Nile. "But oxygen makes dead skin rot. So, if you freeze a body in ice, for instance, it's protected from oxygen and it doesn't go rotten."

"Just like putting a pork chop in the freezer," said Jane.

"The same thing," said Miss Nile. "One mummy of an ice man was found frozen in a glacier in 1991. He'd been there over five thousand years! Once he started to thaw out, they had to put him in a giant fridge to preserve him," said Miss Nile.

"Yikes!" I said. "Imagine going to get a drink of milk and finding *that* in the fridge!"

NATURAL MUMMIES

by Sunny

1. ICE-MAN MUMMY
- found in very cold places like the mountains of Europe. (Also in fridges!)

2. PICKLED MUMMY
- found in peat bogs
- cold marshy places that pickle the body. Skin turns leathery and hard in the water.

3. BAKED MUMMY
- found buried under the hot sand of deserts. Sand dries out the skin and bakes it.

"But, not all mummies were made naturally," said Miss Nile. "Later on, people decided to try to preserve dead bodies on purpose. And, of course, one ancient people became famous for making mummies. Anyone know who?"

"The Egyptians!" said Sean, beating us all to it.

"What? Older than Mr Hedges?" asked Sunny. (Mr Hedges is our headteacher. He must be forty!)

"Much, much older," said Miss Nile. "Ancient Egyptian civilization lasted three thousand years – from around 3000 BC to 30 BC. Even before the Romans came along, the Egyptians had been around for centuries."

Miss Nile crossed to the window and pulled down a map. (I swear it was a blind before, but now it was a map of the world.)

"Egypt is right here at the top of Africa," said Miss Nile, pointing at the map.

"In ancient times, the Egyptians were way ahead of everyone else. Before the Romans were building roads, the Egyptians were doing this..."

Miss Nile let the blind shoot up with a THRING! that woke Queenie, who'd been dozing on the window sill.

We all gasped – instead of our playground outside the window, there was the biggest beach I'd ever seen! There were palm trees along the banks of a wide river, which was busy with strange, banana-shaped boats. Behind the river, I could see buildings – houses, temples and pyramids… It was ancient Egypt!

"Are we going down the river?" asked the twins, Amy and Julie.

"Not yet. Wait till the funeral," said Miss Nile.

We all looked at each other. The funeral? Whose funeral?

But Miss Nile's dancing feet were tapping away again and her bangles were whizzing around like Catherine wheels as she waved her arms about. "The ancient Egyptians were amazing!" she enthused. "And luckily, we can learn an awful lot about them from mummies."

HOW? A MUMMY DOESN'T EXACTLY SAY MUCH.

EVEN WHEN THEY'RE DEAD, BODIES CAN PASS ON A LOT OF INFORMATION. IT'S JUST A CASE OF KNOWING WHERE TO LOOK.

Our teacher crossed to the computer and clicked on the mouse till she reached a website called Marvellous Mummies. A picture of an ancient brown mummy lying in a coffin appeared on the screen.

"Then let's make it bigger," said Miss Nile. She clicked on ENLARGE and the picture started to grow. It doubled in size, then went on getting bigger and bigger and BIGGER. Soon, the picture was off the screen and covering an entire wall of our class. A giant mummy was looking down on us and you could see everything. And I mean *everything* – even the skin and face. The bandages seemed to be see-through!

"*Now* what do you think a mummy can tell you?" asked Miss Nile. "How about some detective work?"

We started to call out lots of ideas and Miss Nile added quite a few of her own. She scribbled them on the wall around the giant picture so that we ended up with the *mummy* of all wall charts.

We were so busy being detectives that we didn't hear the bell go for the end of the

COFFIN WOOD – helps to tell us the age of the mummy.

AMULETS – precious charms wrapped in the linen to ward off evil and protect the mummy. The ancient Egyptians believed in magic!

FLOWERS – tell us about plants that grew thousands of years ago. The ancient Egyptians used many plants in medecine.

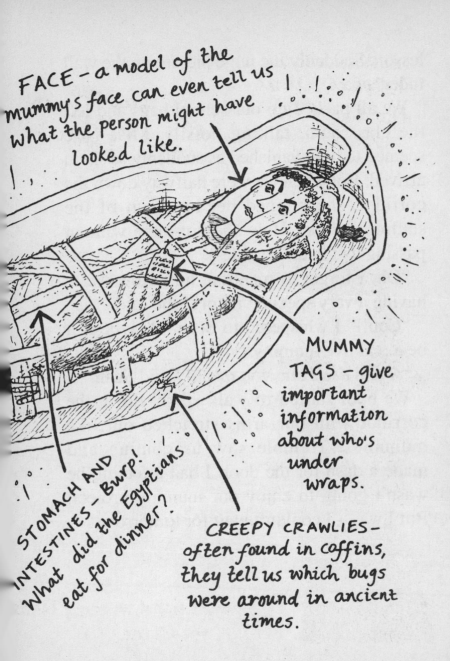

FACE – a model of the mummy's face can even tell us what the person might have looked like.

MUMMY TAGS – give important information about who's under wraps.

STOMACH AND INTESTINES – Burp! What did the Egyptians eat for dinner?

CREEPY CRAWLIES – often found in coffins, they tell us which bugs were around in ancient times.

lesson. Suddenly the huge picture on the wall faded away.

We all packed up our school bags and left the classroom, talking noisily. Miss Nile seemed to have vanished as suddenly as she'd arrived. But when we were halfway down the corridor, she popped her head out of the staffroom door. (How she got there without passing us I hadn't a clue!)

"Oh, I forgot to mention, tomorrow we're having a very special visitor!" she said.

"Cool!" I whispered to Sean. "Maybe it'll be a real live mummy."

"A real *dead* one you mean!" said Sean.

We both started to walk stiffly down the corridor with our arms stretched out like mummies. Tremble saw us coming and made a dash for the door. I had a feeling he wasn't going to enjoy our mummy project. But I was – I couldn't *wait* for tomorrow.

Kiss kiss – it's Pharaoh

"Who can tell me what the ancient Egyptians called their king?" asked Miss Nile at the beginning of our next lesson.

We all shot our hands in the air. This was easy peasy.

"Pharaoh," said Kevin Dobbs. I almost fainted as Oh Kevin hardly ever gets a question right. (He's better known for causing disasters, which is why we call him "Oh Kevin!".)

"Pharaoh, king of all Egypt," said Miss Nile. "And he wasn't any old king either. His people worshipped him."

"You mean like the way I worship Man United?" said Sean.

"Even more than that," laughed Miss Nile. "I mean *really* worship. They thought that the Pharaoh *was* a god."

"But why?" asked Jane.

"You'd better ask him yourself," said Miss Nile. "I promised you a special visitor." Her feet were tapping away excitedly again, but there was a louder noise that sounded almost like the thunder of horses' hooves. In fact, it *was* the thunder of hooves!

Miss Nile opened the door just in time to stop it being knocked off its hinges. In flew a golden chariot pulled by two sleek black horses that were kicking up a cloud of dust. Holding the reins in the chariot was a tall, proud figure.

·58·

He wasn't wearing much, except a white skirt, a stripy towel on his head and a weirdie beard. If you ask me, the beard was a rotten fake – it was held on by something that looked like elastic!

"This is Neffytutu the Ninth, Pharaoh of all Egypt," said Miss Nile.

Neffytutu climbed down and looked down his long nose at us. He had heavy, black make-up round his eyes, which made them look wide and staring.

"Wicked chariot, your royalness," said Sean, obviously hoping for a ride.

Neffytutu glared back at him angrily. It looked like Sean had said something wrong and Miss Nile had to step in quickly.

"You're supposed to call him 'Majesty'," she whispered. "Anything else is very rude. Watch me."

To our amazement, Miss Nile knelt down and kissed the classroom floor in front of Neffytutu's feet. "Welcome, oh mighty Majesty!" she said respectfully.

Neffytutu glowered at the rest of us. It was obvious he wasn't answering any of our questions until we did the same. So we all had to get down and kiss the smelly old classroom floor! (I only pretended, but don't tell anyone.)

Neffytutu now seemed satisfied. He caught sight of Queenie the cat and picked her up in his arms. Normally Queenie's too snooty to let anyone but Miss Nile hold her, but she didn't seem to mind being stroked by royalty!

"Speak," said Neffytutu, grandly. "You may ask a question."

"Miss Nile says you're a god, Majesty" said Jane. "Is that true?"

"Of course," said Neffytutu. "The first rulers of Egypt were the gods who lived on Earth, just like people. The last of the gods to rule was the sky god, Horus. When I became king, his spirit entered me and I became a god, too."

"You mean you're a bit like Superman? Can you see through walls with your X-ray vision?" I asked.

Neffytutu looked at me as if I was bonkers. Perhaps he hadn't heard of Superman.

"Are all Pharaohs made into mummies when they die, Majesty?" asked Sunny.

"Of course," nodded Neffytutu. "Unless I'm mummified, how will my ka recognize my body?"

Sunny looked confused. "What car? I thought you drove a chariot."

"Not that kind of car," explained Miss Nile. "The ka is what the Egyptians called the life force. When you died, your ka came looking for your body. It was important to be mummified, so you didn't rot away before your ka found your body."

Neffytutu nodded as if this was obvious. It all sounded pretty daft to me, but I wasn't about to argue in case he decided to have me executed or something. It didn't stop Kevin though. He always says the first thing that comes into his head.

"Where's your crown?" he demanded suddenly. "Why are you wearing a towel on your head?"

"*Towel*?" said Neffytutu, glaring at Kevin. "You dare to speak of the royal headdress as a *towel*?"

"Um … he *meant* headdress, oh Majesty," said Miss Nile, glancing anxiously at Kevin. "But you do wear a crown for special occasions, don't you?"

"Hold this, I will show you," commanded Neffytutu, handing Miss Nile his stripy headdress. When I looked again, he was wearing a tall red hat. He took it off and another hat appeared in its place! As he swapped his headgear, he explained what they all meant.

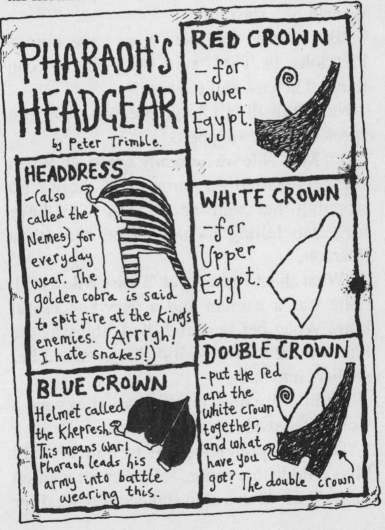

PHARAOH'S HEADGEAR
by Peter Trimble.

RED CROWN
– for Lower Egypt.

HEADDRESS
– (also called the Nemes) for everyday wear. The golden cobra is said to spit fire at the kings enemies. (Arrrgh! I hate snakes!)

WHITE CROWN
– for Upper Egypt.

BLUE CROWN
Helmet called the Khepresh. This means War! Pharaoh leads his army into battle wearing this.

DOUBLE CROWN
– put the red and the white crown together, and what have you got? The double crown

"What about girls?" asked Amy.

"Yes, can they be Pharaohs, too?" said Julie.

"Never!" replied Neffytutu scornfully. "Pharaoh is the son of a god. How can a woman be a son?"

"But it's true that there were *some* women Pharaohs, isn't it?" said Miss Nile. "I can think of at least half a dozen."

Neffytutu didn't look pleased. "Do not speak of it," he snapped.

But Miss Nile was *already* speaking. When she gets started on something, there's no stopping her and she seemed to have forgotten telling us not to be rude to a Pharaoh.

"What about Hatshepsut?" Miss Nile asked. "She was a woman and a very successful king. When her husband died, she was the Pharaoh for twenty years! She even led her soldiers into battle."

"Didn't anyone mind that she was a woman?" asked one of the twins.

"Oh, they pretended not to notice," said Miss Nile with a smile. "Hatshepsut is often shown dressed as a man and people called her

'His Majesty'. She's even pictured with a false beard – just like that one!"

Miss Nile pointed to Neffytutu's weird beard and quickly stopped pointing when she noticed Neffytutu's furious expression. She turned a shade of pink and decided to change the subject.

"Um ... ah, of course," she stammered, "most Pharaohs *were* men and there were lots of famous ones. Why don't we take a look at some of them?"

Miss Nile produced a handful of coins from a pocket.

"Great!" I thought. "I could do with some extra pocket money!"

Our teacher passed the coins round the class, so that we could look at them. I wondered what coins had to do with Pharaohs and found out when I held one. One moment I was looking at the Queen of England, then her face and hair started to change shape in front of my eyes! Suddenly, I was staring at one of the greatest Pharaohs of all time. We passed the coins round, enjoying watching the faces change as we held them. On the other side of the coin you could read all about the Egyptian kings!

FAMOUS PHARAOHS
by Amy and Julie

PEPI II (2246–2152 BC)

The longest reigning king in history. Pepi became Pharaoh aged six and reigned for the next 94 years. It was difficult to find a successor because they all died waiting!

RAMESSES II (1279–1212 BC)

Famous for starting a huge building programme, including the temple at Abu Simbel. Ramesses put his name on other existing buildings to pretend that he'd built them, too!

AKHENATEN (1352–1338 BC)

Banned the worship of all the old Egyptian gods, except the one god Aten. Didn't make him popular. After his death, the city he built was torn down and the old gods restored.

TUTANKHAMUN (1336–1327 BC)

Son of Akhenaten, he was only ten when he became king and may have been murdered at 18. His fabulous tomb was found in 1922 with Tut's mummy inside.

CLEOPATRA VII (51–30 BC)

The Last Pharaoh and another woman (hooray!) Tried to restore Egypt's greatness with the help of the Roman general Mark Antony. When she failed, Cleopatra killed herself.

Neffytutu had been taking a good look at the coins himself.

WHERE IS MY HEAD? WHERE IS THE GREAT NEFFYTUTU THE NINTH?

Miss Nile looked a bit embarrassed. She obviously hadn't got a coin showing our visitor. "Well, there were an awful lot of Pharaohs," she said. "About 170 in all…"

"And you're probably not very famous," added Kevin, helpfully.

Oh, Kevin!

That finally did it. Neffytutu turned purple with rage. He stepped into his chariot and put on his striped royal headdress – the one with the golden cobra. He began to chant something that sounded like a magic spell and we all took a step back, wondering what he was going to do.

"Oh, dear!" said Miss Nile. "I hope you didn't..."

But it was too late. The golden cobra on Neffytutu's headdress was starting to uncurl and come to life!

Miss Nile had to do something quickly or she was toast. She tugged on the horses' reins and immediately they reared up on their hind legs and galloped away. A thick cloud of dust rose into the air and we all waited for the crash as the chariot hit the classroom wall. But when the dust cleared, Neffytutu, his horses and his gleaming chariot had disappeared.

"Oh, well," said Miss Nile. "He was a bit of a big head, wasn't he?"

"No wonder," I said, "with that many hats!"

"Who were those gods he was talking about?" asked Sean. "Horace or something?"

Miss Nile laughed. "I think you mean Horus. Maybe it's time we met *all* of the gods."

There was a loud roll of thunder…

"Help!" yelped Tremble. "What's happening now?"

Ye gods!

Suddenly, the lights went off and we were in pitch darkness. The only sound I could hear was Tremble's knees knocking together. I must admit, I wasn't feeling too brave myself – especially after the blinding flash of lightning. In the bright light, I saw Miss Nile and, behind her, a line of huge monsters with the heads of birds, baboons and crocodiles! I tried to run away, but the rest of the class had the same idea and we all bumped into each other in the dark.

"Relax! There's nothing to be scared of," said Miss Nile. "They're not real. Look!"

The darkness was now lit by flaming candles in bowls. I could see that the monsters were nothing more than life-size paintings on a wall.

OOOPS! DID I STEP ON YOUR TOE?

"Where are we?" asked the twins, both at the same time.

"We're in a temple to the gods," said Miss Nile. Her feet were starting to dance again. "I wanted to show you this wall painting. Isn't it fantastic?"

We had to admit that it was. But it was pretty spooky, too, with candles casting shadows all round the walls.

"Who are those weirdos?" asked Kevin.

"They're the gods," explained Miss Nile. "That one's called Anubis."

"Ugly or what!" said Jane. "Why's he got a dog's head?"

"It's the head of a jackal," said Miss Nile. "A jackal is a type of wild dog. Anubis was often shown like that. In fact, the Egyptians pictured many of their gods as animals, birds or insects."

"Why?" I asked. "Didn't they know what they looked like?"

"I admit it can get a little confusing. Take the goddess Hathor. Sometimes she's shown as a cow or as a woman. On the other hand, she might be a woman with the head or the ears of a cow."

"My head hurts already," groaned Kevin.

"Don't worry," grinned Miss Nile. "There are around two thousand gods, so it's easy to get them mixed up. Some are only household gods or local gods – the ones to remember are the powerful gods worshipped by everyone."

"Which ones are they?" asked Jane.

"Take a look around you," said Miss Nile, pointing to the temple walls.

We turned and saw that the Egyptian gods were looking down on us – rows and rows of them. It made me feel kind of creepy. But that was nothing compared with how I felt when I saw a god put a hand to his mouth and yawn! The next thing I knew, the paintings started to turn their heads towards us. They stretched their arms and legs. Their bodies rippled like water and the gods began to peel themselves off the wall, one by one!

I would have run if I could have moved, but Tremble was holding on to me for dear life.

"Miss Nile, p-p-please can I be excused!"
he said.

"It's all right, Peter. They won't hurt you,"
said Miss Nile. That was easy for her to say,
our teacher was obviously used to meeting
someone with the head of crocodile.

Miss Nile turned to the nearest god, who
had a tall hat with even taller feathers growing
out of it. "Let's see, you must be Re the Sun
God. Am I right?"

"Amon Re, so great they named me twice,"
the god replied. "As you know, I'm king of

the gods. None of the others are really worth bothering with."

"Oh, pleeease!" sighed the god next to him, going green (or was he green before?). "If anyone's important, I'd say it's the king of the dead."

"Ah, you're Osiris, god of the underworld," said Miss Nile.

"My husband," said a tall, dark-haired goddess, pushing to the front.

I AM ISIS – GREAT MOTHER AND THE ONLY GODDESS YOU REALLY NEED TO KNOW.

HA!

This started a terrible uproar among the gods and goddesses. Soon, they were all squabbling over who was the most important. Feathers flew from a winged goddess and the crocodile god kept snapping at everyone. Things only simmered down when a tiny bearded god accidentally sat on a candle. He danced around, clutching his bottom, which made all the gods laugh.

"That's Bes – jester to the gods," explained Miss Nile.

"They don't act much like gods, do they?" I whispered. "Shouldn't they be more, you know, godly?"

Miss Nile shrugged. "The Egyptians treated their gods much like people. For instance, they had to be woken up every morning."

"They sang to us," smiled Isis. "It was very soothing."

"They had to be fed and entertained, too," said Miss Nile. "Sometimes, they fought and argued just like humans."

"But why did they need so *many* gods?" asked Jane.

It was Amun Re who answered. "To look after the Earth, of course. Each of us was in charge of something – the sun, the moon, healing…"

"Everything was in our power," interrupted Osiris. "If you wanted good crops, you prayed to us. Even Pharaoh had to keep us happy. Every day, his priests brought us presents in the temple – they dressed our statues in new clothes and applied make-up."

"But what did gods actually DO?" asked Jane.

"We ruled!" said Amon Re. "And, of course, we were there to help people. If they had a problem or question, they would bring it to us."

"Like what?" asked the twins together.

"Anything you wanted to know," said Miss Nile. "Let's try it. Everyone write down a question on a piece of paper and we'll ask the gods for the answer."

This sounded like fun. I wrote, "Will there be pizza for lunch?"

Sean wrote, "Has Miss Nile got a boyfriend?" and showed it to me, giggling.

Then we handed in our questions and Miss Nile picked one out. She unfolded the piece of paper:

Which of you is the god of the mummies?

"Good question," Miss Nile said.

I saw Tina Molina blush, which meant it was her question.

The god with the jackal's head stepped forward. "I am the god of embalming," he growled in a deep voice.

"Remember Anubis?" said Miss Nile. "The Egyptians told lots of stories about the gods – one tells how Anubis came to make the very first mummy."

"Great!" said Sunny. "Would you tell us the story?"

We all nodded our heads eagerly.

Osiris looked offended. "I should tell it. It's my story!"

"And mine," said Isis. "If it wasn't for me, *you* wouldn't be here to tell the tale."

"What about me?" growled Anubis.

It looked like another argument was brewing, but Amon Re held up his hand for silence. "We'll ALL tell the story," he said. "In fact, we'll do better than that – we'll perform it for you."

"You mean, like a play?" I said. I'd never seen a play performed by gods.

"Yes, we'll show you *The Story of Osiris and Isis*," said Amon Re. "I will be the narrator."

We sat down on the floor to watch. This was going to be good. Amon Re clapped his hands and the temple was plunged into darkness.

"Oooh!" we all cried. It was just like going to a pantomime – only better!

Like footlights on a stage, a row of candles flickered into life. A mysterious red curtain swished back and Amun Re began to speak...

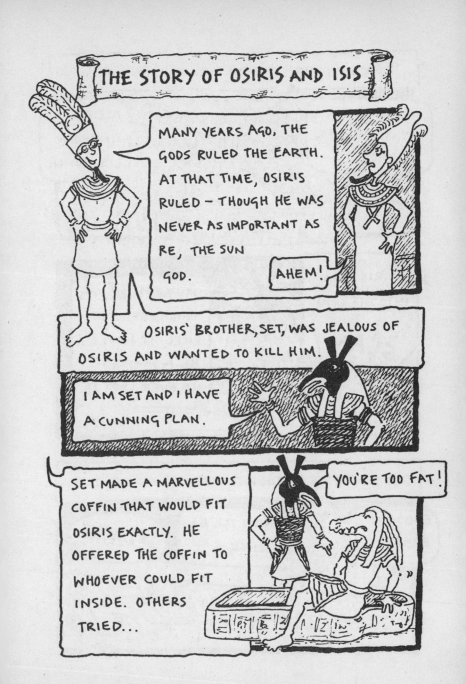

49

51

THEN ISIS BREATHED LIFE BACK INTO OSIRIS.

AND THE MIGHTY SUN GOD, RE, MADE OSIRIS KING OF THE UNDERWORLD.

WHICH PROVES THAT GREAT GODS NEVER GO TO PIECES!

CLAP CLAP

"What a weird story! Is it true?" asked Kevin.

"Well, the ancient Egyptians believed it," said Miss Nile. "They told lots of stories about their gods – just like the Greeks and the Romans. It was their way of explaining the world they lived in."

"And did Anubis really make the first mummy?" I asked.

Miss Nile smiled. "It's a good story, but it's more likely that the Egyptians got the idea from bodies that were preserved when they were buried in the desert. Once rich people started to be buried in tombs, the hot sand didn't preserve them any more. So they had to find a new way to make mummies."

"And they called it embalming!" said Jane.

"Personally, I prefer the story of Osiris and Isis," I said.

I turned to thank the gods for their play, but they were all back on the walls – looking as lifeless as statues. Miss Nile snuffed out the candles and, quick as a flash, we were back in our classroom at Pickle Hill.

You can find out more about the gods for your homework," said Miss Nile. "And, next lesson, we'll find out what mummies are really made of!"

Sean's Guide to the Glorious Gods

← OSIRIS
God and ruler of the dead who meets you in the afterlife.
Dead important!

ISIS →
Wife of Osiris. Mother goddess and goddess of crafts.

← ANUBIS
Mummy-making god of embalmers.

SET →
God of the desert, chaos and evil.

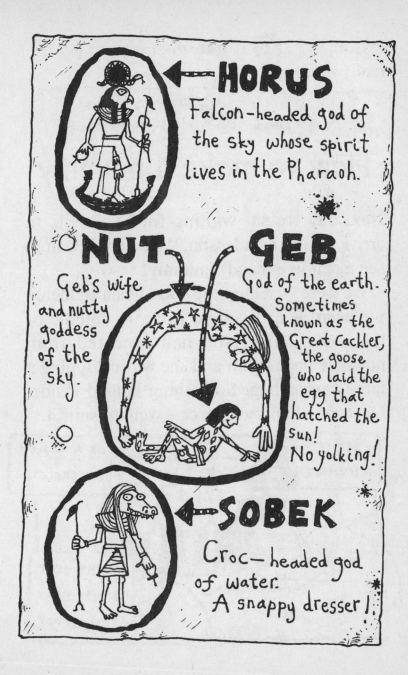

HORUS

Falcon-headed god of the sky whose spirit lives in the Pharaoh.

NUT

Geb's wife and nutty goddess of the sky.

GEB

God of the earth. Sometimes known as the Great Cackler, the goose who laid the egg that hatched the sun! No yolking!

SOBEK

Croc-headed god of water. A snappy dresser!

How to make a mummy

Next day we sat waiting for Miss Nile to arrive for our next lesson. We couldn't wait to see a real live (dead) mummy!

We were watching the door, when suddenly we heard a ZIP! sound from the middle of the room. Miss Nile had appeared from nowhere once again and she was unzipping a large canvas bag. Something bulged inside. Queenie – hungry as ever – went to sniff it.

"Now," said Miss Nile, scratching her head. "What did I do with the instructions?" She reached into the bag, which suddenly sprang to life with a snapping sound. Everyone jumped, especially Queenie, who was sitting on top of it. The thing in the bag had assembled itself as if by magic.

Miss Nile rescued Queenie from the top of the tent, where the cat was hanging on by her claws.

"Poor Queenie," she soothed. "Did that nasty old tent give you a fright?"

I sniffed. "Pooh! It's smells a bit ancient."

"It would do. It's three thousand years old," said Miss Nile with a grin. "You're looking at an ancient Egyptian tent."

"Where are the sides?" asked Sunny.

"There aren't any – and you'll soon see why," said Miss Nile. "Come on, let's take a look inside."

We could all see what was inside the tent – our classroom floor – but we followed Miss Nile just the same. Inside, the air was hotter, as if we were in a desert. Flies buzzed. Then the terrible stink hit us!

"Phew! What's that rotten pong?" asked Kevin, holding his nose.

"Dead bodies, I would imagine," said Miss Nile with a smile. "You wanted to see a mummy, so we've come to the embalmers. Now you see why the tent sides are open and we're out in the desert."

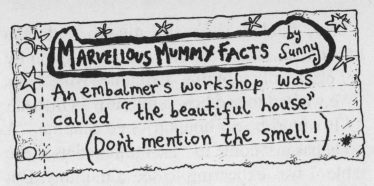

MARVELLOUS MUMMY FACTS by Sunny

An embalmer's workshop was called "the beautiful house". (Don't mention the smell!)

We looked outside and saw that Miss Nile was right. We were far from any houses, surrounded only by sand and red mountains. As we moved back inside the tent, we bumped into three ancient Egyptians, bent over a table. Goodness knows where they came from!

A tall, bald man turned round and bowed.

SHARMA, CHIEF EMBALMER, HUMBLY AT YOUR SERVICE. YOU'D LIKE TO MUMMIFY YOUR CAT?

MIAOW!

"No, thanks! She's still alive!" said Tina hastily.

"We're only looking," explained Miss Nile. "We wanted to see how a mummy is made."

"It would be an honour," said Sharma. "A body has just come in." He motioned us to the table. I was expecting to see a mummy. But instead there was a dead Egyptian laid out, practically naked!

LUCKY THEY LEFT HIM A TOWEL!

Tremble looked like he was going to faint. "Is he really d-d-dead?" he gasped.

"I certainly hope so – I don't want him walking off!" said Sharma cheerfully. "His name was Manetho. Luckily, he was rich, so he'll have a good mummy."

"What if he'd been poor?" asked Jane.

"We'd do a cheap job and sew him up quickly," shrugged Sharma. "Mind you, I'm always careful. I know of a queen who was stuffed so badly her cheeks exploded. Boof!"

One of the embalmers was laying out Sharma's instruments on the table. There were some sharp-looking knives, some pots of sweet, smelly ointment and a long hook about the thickness of a knitting needle. Sunny picked up the hook.

"Are you going to knit him a jumper?" joked Sunny.

"Who is a jumper? This is for removing the brain," said Sharma. "I'll show you." He took the needle from Sunny and poked it right up the body's nose.

"Ow!" said Sunny, looking away.

None of us could bear to look, except Miss Nile. She was watching with fascination.

"What's he doing now?" asked Jane, her hands over her eyes.

"Pulling the brain out through the nose," said Miss Nile. "The Egyptians didn't think the brain was important, so they threw it away."

"Now for the stomach," said Sharma. "Anyone like to help?"

Funnily enough, none of us did.

Sharma took a sharp knife and made a cut up one side of the body. Then he slipped in his hand and felt around. "Now where…? Ah, got it," he said.

"Got what?" asked Tina Molina.

"The stomach!" Sharma said. We all turned away from the table before he could show us. Miss Nile might have warned us that mummy-making was so revolting!

"They take out all the organs except the heart," she explained. "Then, the lungs, the liver, the stomach and intestines are all buried with the mummy, just in case the owner needs them in the next life."

Miss Nile pointed out four strange-looking jars with animal-shaped heads that were under the table.

"Oh, aren't they cute?" cooed Tina Molina, picking one up. "This one looks like a little monkey!"

"Yes, they're canopic jars," explained Miss Nile. "You see, there are four. One each for the liver, lungs, stomach and intestines." Tina put the jar down quickly. She'd suddenly turned a shade of green.

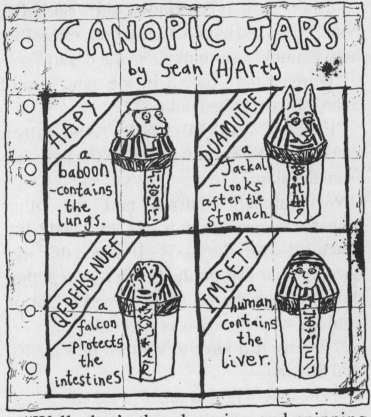

CANOPIC JARS

by Sean (H)Arty

HAPY
a baboon -contains the lungs.

DUAMUTEF
a Jackal -looks after the stomach.

QEBEHSENUEF
a falcon -protects the intestines

IMSETY
a human, contains the liver.

"Well, that's the chopping and snipping finished," said Sharma. "Now we have to dry out the body."

"How do you do that – hang it on a washing line?" asked Kevin.

"No, no, we use this," said Sharma. He lifted a bag on to the table. Inside was a fine powder.

"It looks like salt!" said Sean.

"You're right, it *is* a kind of salt!" said Miss Nile. "It's called natron. Can anyone remember how mummies were made in the desert?"

"Weren't they baked in the sand?" said Sean. "Like a baked potato?"

"Exactly!" said Miss Nile. "And natron works just like sand. It soaks up the moisture from the skin."

We watched Sharma and the other embalmers take handfuls of natron and pat it down all over the body. It was a bit like burying your dad on the beach – except they didn't stop at the neck! They went right on until the whole body was covered.

"Now we just have to wait till he's ready," said Sharma.

"How long will that take?" I asked.

"About forty days," the embalmer replied.

"*Forty*!" I said. "That's weeks and weeks!"

"Don't worry ... here's one I prepared earlier!" said Sharma, disappearing through a tent flap.

We followed him and saw another body. At least, I *think* it was a body – it looked more like a zombie from a horror film… It's skin was dark and blotchy and the legs were as thin as lolly sticks.

"Surely you won't bury him like that?" asked Jane.

"Of course not," said Sharma. "This is where an embalmer really shows his skill. A bit of stuffing, some oils and make-up and he'll look as good as new."

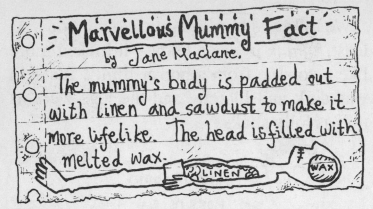

Marvellous Mummy Fact

by Jane MacJane.

The mummy's body is padded out with linen and sawdust to make it more lifelike. The head is filled with melted wax.

LINEN

WAX

Sharma set to work. He even borrowed some of Miss Nile's make-up and was very impressed with her lipstick. Finally, the body was ready to be bandaged.

I THINK YOU GOT CARRIED AWAY WITH THE MAKE-UP!

"This is my favourite part!" Sharma told us. "Who would like to learn how to wrap up a mummy?"

We *all* wanted to try – since it didn't involve anything yucky. Sharma brought out lots of rolls of linen. And I mean lots!

THERE'S MILES OF IT!

ACTUALLY, ABOUT 375 SQUARE METRES.
EGYPTIANS HAD TO SAVE LINEN ALL THEIR
LIVES FOR THEIR MUMMIES!

Sharma showed us how to wrap the body carefully in linen, starting with the fingers and toes. Inside the layers we placed jewels and amulets – lucky charms to protect the body from evil. Finally, the mummy was finished. It looked like a lumpy brown parcel.

"A thousand thanks!" said Sharma. "And now I have an important priest arriving. Dead, of course. If you'll excuse me…"

He bowed and disappeared through a tent flap. An embalmer always seemed to be busy. Miss Nile told us it was a highly respected job in ancient Egypt. Everyone needed the services of the embalmer sooner or later. All the same, it's not a job I fancy myself…

The sun was sinking red in the sky as we stepped outside the tent – and found ourselves right back in our classroom.

"That was amazing," I said. "I never knew so much went into making a mummy."

"Or came out!" joked Sunny.

"Can I look now?" asked Tremble. We all laughed. He was *still* covering his eyes with his hands!

At that moment, the bell rang and Miss Nile looked at her watch. "Ah, we're just in time for lunch," she said. "I do hope it's not liver and onions."

All of a sudden, I didn't feel that hungry.

Marvellous Mummy Facts
by Amy and Julie

The Egyptians made millions of mummies. Years later, many were dug up and used in all sorts of weird ways! Seventeenth-century doctors thought that eating minced-up mummy would cure broken bones! Victorians kept a mummy's foot or a hand in a glass case on the mantelpiece.

Let's hold a funeral!

Next morning, Miss Nile announced, "We'd better go now or we'll miss the funeral."

"Whose funeral?" said Tremble, looking anxious. "And where are we going?"

"You'll soon see," said Miss Nile. She opened her hand to show us a brown husk as small as a thumbnail.

"Anyone know what this is?" she asked. "I'll give you a clue. It's a type of ear."

"Funny-looking ear," said Kevin. "Looks more like a seed."

"I know – it's an ear of corn!" I guessed. (Sometimes, I'm quite bright.)

"Right," said Miss Nile. "Let's see what happens when we plant it."

She dropped the ear of corn on a brown rug in front of her desk. At least, last time I looked it was a rug. Now, it had turned into a patch of earth. What happened next was a bit like watching the magic beans grow in *Jack and the Beanstalk*. Green shoots poked out of the rug and started growing upwards. First, there were one or two, then hundreds of them. Soon, they were spreading into the whole classroom. In no time at all, the shoots reached our waists and had turned a golden colour.

Miss Nile was already striding off across the field. "Come on. It's this way!" she called. Our classroom had vanished and we were in a landscape of golden cornfields. The corn waved in the breeze.

"Is this where they're holding the funeral?" I asked.

"Not far now," said Miss Nile. "First, I wanted you to see the ancient Egyptian idea of heaven."

"A field?" said Sunny. "Isn't that a bit corny?" We all groaned.

"Look around," said Miss Nile. "What does this place look like?"

We all looked. The sky was blue, the birds were singing and we could see some Egyptian workers in the next field, harvesting the corn.

"Much the same as Egypt, if you ask me," said Jane.

"It *is* Egypt!" said Miss Nile. "The Egyptians believed that the next world would be just like their own country – only better. The sun would shine, the crops would grow and everyone would have plenty to eat. They called it the Field of Reeds."

"Did everyone go to heaven, then?" asked Tremble.

"They hoped so," said Miss Nile. "But it was a dangerous journey to get there. Your mummy had to pass through the underworld, avoiding demons and lakes of fire."

Tremble stopped in his tracks. "We're not going to see *them*, are we?"

I could feel a breeze on my face and hear the sound of water up ahead. We came out of the cornfield and stood on the banks of a river.

"The River Nile!" said Miss Nile.

FUNNY PLACE FOR A FUNERAL. WON'T EVERYONE GET WET?

"The Nile was Egypt's main road," explained Miss Nile. "All the traffic passed down here – even funerals! Oh, and by the way, you might want to keep an eye out for crocodiles. They sometimes hide among the reeds."

Crocodiles? She might have mentioned it before! Tremble put up his hand, but then remembered that there was nowhere to be excused to.

The next thing we heard was a terrible sound of moaning and wailing. It sounded like Queenie with her tail trapped in a door! But the sound was coming from the river and it was getting louder.

"What's that horrible noise?" asked Sunny.

"The funeral," said Miss Nile, pointing. "Here it comes now."

At that moment, a long, pointed boat passed by. It was so loaded up, I was surprised it didn't sink. In the middle of the boat, under a kind of tent, was a golden coffin shaped like a person!

"But why are they all making that terrible row?" I asked.

A Pharaoh's Funeral Barge

Two oars to steer

Canopy

Pharaoh's mummy in its coffin

Priest reading spells and prayers

Wooden barge known as a barque

Wailing mourners

by Sammy

"It's their job, Sammy," explained Miss Nile. "Women were paid to mourn at funerals by weeping and wailing. The more mourners you had, the more important you were."

"With that racket, it must be someone pretty big," said Kevin.

"It is," said Miss Nile. "Remember our Pharaoh friend, Neffytutu?"

"You mean that's *him* in the coffin?" I asked.

"Yes… Unfortunately, he choked on a date stone. Still, I thought you'd like to take part in his funeral."

"Miss! What do you mean – take part?" asked Sean.

Looking down, I saw that my shoes had vanished. I was dressed like an ancient Egyptian, wearing only a linen skirt and a wide, coloured necklace! I felt a bit daft, until I noticed that the rest of the class were all dressed like Egyptians, too.

The twins were busy admiring each other's make-up, and Kevin couldn't work out where to put his hands now he didn't have any pockets to stuff them into.

Before we had time to think, the funeral barge had landed on our bank.

The chief priest, dressed in a leopard skin, seemed to be expecting us. So, we joined the procession, with Miss Nile telling us what to do.

"You twins can be the two Kites," she said.

"Great!" said Sunny. "I've always wanted to see Julie fly!"

We all laughed and got a lot of dirty looks.

"Remember, it's a funeral," Miss Nile whispered. "It's not meant to be funny. The Kites are the chief wailers – they represent the goddesses Isis and Nephthys, so it's a great honour to be chosen."

The twins proudly took their places behind Neffytutu's coffin.

Tremble had to walk at the front of the procession, sprinkling milk as he went.

Sean's job was to swing a smoking pot of smelly stuff called incense. He swung it around so enthusiastically, we all started to choke and cough.

Finally, the procession was ready to set off – except that someone needed to help pull the sledge carrying the Pharaoh's coffin. And guess who got that job? Yes – me and Oh Kevin!

Another sledge came behind, carrying the canopic jars that held the Pharaoh's organs.

The mourners had also brought a jumble of fans, wigs, food and furniture to bury with him. Neffytutu obviously planned to be comfortable in the next life!

It was the noisiest funeral on Earth! What with the women wailing and the priest chanting, they should have supplied us with earplugs!

Miss Nile was having a whale of a time.

She was dressed as an Egyptian princess and had nothing to carry but Queenie, seated on a cushion.

"How far have we got to go?" I whispered. The funeral sledge weighed a tonne and the sun was blistering the back of my neck. And, to make matters worse, Kevin kept treading on my heels.

"There it is up ahead," said Miss Nile.

We halted at a doorway cut into the rock of the cliff. "This is the Valley of Kings," our teacher told us. "Around 60 Pharaohs are buried here in tombs deep under the cliffs."

Slowly, we dragged the Pharaoh's coffin down into the tomb. There, we stood it on one end so that it was upright. It was dark and the chamber was crowded with people. The incense got right up my nose.

Suddenly, a leopard stepped out of the shadows and gave us all a fright.

"It's only the priest in his leopard skin," explained Miss Nile in a whisper. "They're going to perform the Opening of the Mouth ceremony. Shhh! I've always wanted to see this!"

We edged closer to watch what was happening. It was dead spooky – in the half-light, the golden face of the coffin looked almost real. The priest was touching it with a kind of snake-shaped wand.

"What's he doing now – some sort of magic trick?" I whispered.

"Good guess," whispered Miss Nile. "It's a spell to bring the mummy back to life. The priest touches the mouth so that the mummy will be able to speak and eat in the tomb."

It was at that moment the disaster happened. We were all pressed in close to see the coffin and the incense must have been too much for Kevin. Suddenly, he gave a loud sneeze and banged his head on the nearest object. It was a pity it was the Pharaoh's coffin.

For a second, the box swayed dangerously. Then it fell forwards with a deafening crash.

The priest and the mourners stared at Kevin in horror. Some of the guards reached for their swords. As we backed towards the entrance they started to close in on us menacingly.

"Er … this might be a good time to leave," murmured Miss Nile. "When I count to three, run as fast as you can. Three!"

We all turned and moved like greased lightning. Luckily, once we'd clambered out of the tomb, it vanished.

Somehow, we were safely back at Pickle Hill Primary…

Tomb with a view

"Well, that was exciting, wasn't it?" said Miss Nile, back in our classroom.

"Exciting?" said Sean. "Kevin nearly got us all mummified!"

"How did I know that the coffin was going to fall over?" complained Kevin. "I hardly touched it."

"No harm done," smiled Miss Nile. "And at least we got a glimpse of a Pharaoh's tomb."

"It was dead spooky," said Jane. "I didn't know it would be underground."

Miss Nile picked up Queenie and gave her a stroke. "Of course, not all Pharaohs were buried in the Valley of Kings," she said. "Some of the Old Kingdom kings built the most amazing tombs. You could say they had a real *point* to them."

"Point?" I said. "What do you mean?"

"I'll show you," said Miss Nile, producing a piece of paper and starting to fold it. Her bangles jingled together as her fingers moved in a blur of speed.

Miss Nile had made a perfect pyramid out of paper.

"You mean, they buried Pharaohs in the pyramids?" I said.

"Certainly," said Miss Nile. "The Pharaohs wanted to be buried in style and you can't get much more stylish than a huge pyramid. Of course, they didn't get the idea right away, The first tombs were called mastabas. They were little more than boxes made from mud bricks." She flattened her paper pyramid to show us a rectangular box.

"But then, around 2620 BC," Miss Nile continued, "a clever minister called Imhotep had an idea. If he built lots of smaller mastabas on top of each other, what would he get?"

"Very tired!" said Sean.

"A pyramid!" said Jane. "You mean it would look a bit like steps?"

"Exactly. And that's how Imhotep invented the world's first pyramid. Rather like this…" With a flourish Miss Nile showed us her piece of folded paper, which now looked like a miniature pyramid with lots of tiny steps.

"Wicked!" said Sean.

"Do all pyramids look like that?" asked Julie.

"Not all of them," said Miss Nile. "They come in three different shapes. The step pyramid, the true pyramid and – my personal favourite – the bent pyramid."

"Why was it bent?" I asked.

"Because the Pharaoh had a bent nose!" suggested Sunny.

"No, it was a mistake!" laughed Miss Nile. "The builders got their calculations in a twist and ended up with a bent top. The Pharaoh, Sneferu, wasn't very chuffed, so they had to start again from scratch and build a true pyramid nearby.

"What's the biggest pyramid in the world?" Sunny wanted to know.

"Good question!" said Miss Nile. "It's the Great Pyramid of Giza. You can still go and see it in Egypt today. Can anyone guess how big it is?"

"As big as a bus!" said Sunny.

"As big as our school!" I said

"As big as my dad," suggested Kevin.

"Much, *much* bigger," smiled Miss Nile. "It's 138 metres high. That's taller than the

Statue of Liberty in New York or St Paul's Cathedral in London."

We all tried to imagine something that big but it was too mind-boggling.

Miss Nile stood up, forgetting that Queenie was on her lap and dumping her on the floor.

"To give you an idea how big that is, the Great Pyramid used over two *million* blocks of stone," she said.

"You mean, like two million bricks?" asked Julie.

"Oh, no, Amy, not bricks – much bigger!" said Miss Nile.

There was a cracking sound overhead and flakes of plaster started to fall off the ceiling.

WATCH OUT! THE ROOF'S FALLING IN!

Tina and Jane jumped out of the way just in time to see a block of stone crash into the middle of the room. It was gigantic! Miss Nile went over and patted it as if it was perfectly normal for giant blocks of stone to land in her classroom. "When I say two million, I mean two million blocks this size," she said. "Each one of these stones weighs as much as two and a half elephants."

"That's amazing!" said Kevin. "Where did they find half an elephant?"

We all fell about laughing.

"And don't forget that they didn't have trucks or cranes to help them move the stones," Miss Nile went on.

"How did they lift them then – with elephants?" asked Jane.

"No – with people power," Miss Nile replied. "During the flood season, thousands of Egyptians left their jobs and worked on the Pharaoh's tomb."

"I still can't imagine it," said Sean. "How did they shift two million blocks like this?"

Miss Nile tapped her feet excitedly. "It's one of the great wonders of the world and we're only just starting to understand how the ancient Egyptians did it. They began by drawing a perfect square by the base…"

She used a piece of chalk to scrawl pictures on the side of the block of stone. But, being Pickle Hill, it wasn't a normal diagram. As Miss Nile drew the little figures of workers, they came to life and began to move. Soon, swarms of people were moving across the face of the block in teams.

"Wow!" said Tina. "They look like ants building a nest!"

HOW TO BUILD A GREAT PYRAMID

by Miss Nile

It took up to 100,000 of Pharaoh's workers to build his tomb.

Workers use rounded stone to rub the outer surface smooth.

Stones are dragged up ramps of sand and rubble by teams of workers.

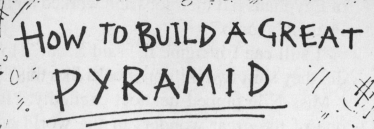

The capstone has to be levered into place.

The pyramid is covered in huge white limestone blocks.

The great pyramid took 20 years to complete.

Miss Nile paused to let the chalk cool down. "So, here's the million-dollar question," she said. "Why a pyramid shape? Why not make them square, rectangular or even egg-shaped?"

I hadn't thought about that. In fact, we were *all* stumped. Even megabrain Jane didn't know.

"Don't worry," laughed Miss Nile. "Not even our top scientists know the answer to that one. Our best guess is that a pyramid was like a giant stairway to heaven. The Pharaoh could climb it and join the sun god in the sky."

One thing still puzzled me. "But why did they stop building them?" I asked. "Why did the ancient Egyptians start putting their tombs under the ground?"

"Good question, Sammy," said Miss Nile. "The only trouble with pyramids is that you can't miss them. And everyone knew what was buried inside."

"The mummy!" said Sean.

"Not just a mummy. Gold and jewels – all the treasures that Pharaohs took into the afterlife. Imagine what a temptation that was!"

"You mean people tried to *steal* them?" asked Jane, shocked.

"I'm afraid so," nodded Miss Nile. "Tomb robbers were a real menace in ancient Egypt. Naturally, pyramids didn't have their doors wide open. The entrance was blocked with huge stones that were packed so close together you couldn't get a hand between them. But that didn't stop the robbers."

Kevin's eyes were goggling. "How did they break in?"

"You'll have to wait till the next lesson to find out," smiled Miss Nile. She was packing up her bag when I leaned over to speak to Sean. When I looked back, she'd disappeared again. "Where did she go?" I asked.

"Search me," said Sean.

Queenie jumped on to Miss Nile's desk and picked up a piece of paper in her mouth.

"Look, she wants us to read it," said Tina.

It said:

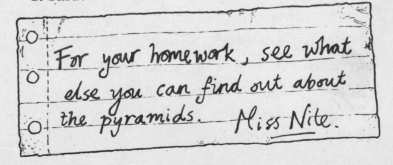

For your homework, see what else you can find out about the pyramids. — Miss Nite.

Popular Pyramids

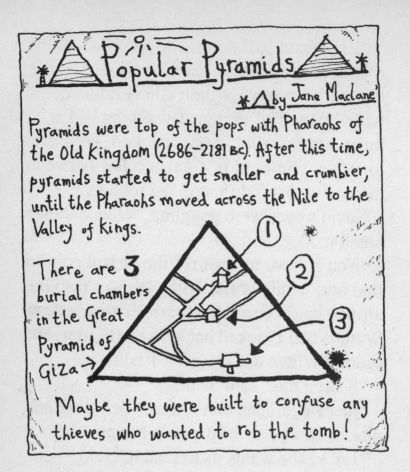

＊△ by Jane Maclane

Pyramids were top of the pops with Pharaohs of the Old Kingdom (2686-2181 BC). After this time, pyramids started to get smaller and crumbier, until the Pharaohs moved across the Nile to the Valley of Kings.

There are **3** burial chambers in the Great Pyramid of Giza →

① ② ③

Maybe they were built to confuse any thieves who wanted to rob the tomb!

Pet mummies

Miss Nile was late arriving for our next lesson, but she'd left something on her desk for us. It looked like a tall vase, but the top had pointed ears and a painted face, just like a cat's. The vase was covered with a criss-cross pattern. Queenie arched her back and hissed at it. She didn't like strange cats on her territory.

But the vase cat just sat there, staring ahead with its painted eyes, not making a sound.

"You don't think it's a *real* cat, do you?" asked Tremble.

"Don't be daft. Where are its legs?" said Sean.

"They could be inside these bandages…" I said. Bandages? Suddenly we all *knew* it wasn't a vase.

Tina Molina gave a shriek. "It's a cat mummy!"

Queenie stared at the mummified cat with wide eyes. Maybe she was wondering if she'd end up like that one day!

"How cruel!" said Tina.

"Not to the Egyptians, it was perfectly natural," said a voice behind us. Miss Nile had suddenly appeared, just as if she'd walked through the wall. We all turned to look at her.

"But why mummify a poor moggy?" asked Amy.

"Well, if you were going to live in the next world, you'd want your favourite pet with you," said Miss Nile. "The Egyptians put their furniture into their tomb, so why not a cat or a dog, too?"

"Did the Egyptians keep tortoises?" asked Tina. (Tina's pet tortoise is called Hercules, though I've never seen him lift anything heavier than a lettuce leaf.)

"I'm not sure about tortoises, but they did mummify some surprising animals!" said Miss Nile. She held out one of the gold bangles on her arm and showed it to us. I'd never looked at it closely before, but now I could see that the bangle was beautifully carved with all kinds of animals.

"This was given to me by an old Egyptian friend," said Miss Nile. "It's over three thousand years old. You would have found all these animals in ancient Egypt."

I could see ordinary pets like dogs and cats, but there were also gazelles, ducks and monkeys. (No tortoises though.) Miss Nile turned the bracelet on her arm and, as it moved, so did the animals! Throwing back their heads, they barked, miaowed and chattered at the tops of their voices.

"They almost look real!" I said.

I pointed to the monkey, which was whooping and showing its teeth. I got a shock when it bit my finger! I yelped and jumped backwards, making Miss Nile drop her bangle in surprise. The gold bracelet spun in circles on her desk with a loud ringing noise.

"Oh, dear…" she said. "I shouldn't have done that."

"Look!" said Amy. The animals were jumping off the bracelet and, more alarming

still, they were now full-size. Soon, there were cats, dogs, monkeys and gazelles running everywhere! It was like a zoo!

Miss Nile shrugged her shoulders and smiled. "Well, it's a good chance to meet some Egyptian animals, I suppose," she laughed. "See what you can find out!"

The twins were examining a thin, grey cat. Queenie sniffed at it and stuck her nose in the air with a look of disgust.

"The Egyptians were the first to keep cats as pets," said Miss Nile. "In fact, they liked them so much, they would treat their furry friend like one of the family."

"But what's so special about cats?" asked Sean.

"They were sacred, which meant they were special to the gods," Miss Nile said. "There was even a cat goddess called Bastet."

BASTET FACT FILE
by Tina Molina

NAME: Bastet, Goddess of cats, daughter of the sun god Re.

TALENTS: Protector of the Pharaohs. Brought the healing power of the sun to ripen crops and heal sickness. If Egyptians wanted to have children, they prayed to Bastet and brought her a basket of kittens. Bastet's temples were one big cat home!

POPULARITY: Bastet liked to party. She had her own festival, with music, dancing and drinking.

"Hear that, Queenie?" said Tina. "You've got your own goddess!"

Queenie tossed her head as if she'd always known she was divine. She jumped up on to Miss Nile's lap, purring loudly.

"Oh, Queenie!" soothed Miss Nile. "Was that sneaky cat getting all the attention?"

It sounded like it was Tremble who wanted our attention. He'd leapt on to a table and was yelling. "Help! Somebody! Heeelp!"

"Don't be silly, Peter," said Sunny. "A little cat's not going to hurt you."

"It's not a cat..." trembled Peter.

"Ah, yes... Did I mention that the Egyptians sometimes kept crocodiles as honoured guests?" asked Miss Nile.

"They're not guests, they *eat* people!" cried Tremble.

"How can it eat you?" laughed Sean. "It's only a baby croc!"

The crocodile was snapping at Tremble's feet as they dangled over the end of the desk. Miss Nile did her best to catch hold of its tail. But the crocodile didn't want to be caught. I *would* have helped, but I didn't fancy getting near the sharp end with the teeth!

"How did ancient Egyptians keep crocodiles in their houses?" I asked.

"They didn't," Miss Nile panted. "They were kept at temples and fed by the priests. Sometimes, people even dressed the crocodiles in jewellery."

"I thought you said that crocodiles were dangerous. Didn't they attack people?" asked Sean.

"Oh, yes," said Miss Nile. "Crocodiles and hippos were a constant danger to boats on the Nile. That's probably why the Egyptians tried to make friends with them. By worshipping the crocodile god, Sobek, they thought he would protect them."

By now, Tina was patting a dog, while the gazelle was chewing the bottom of the curtains.

"Time these animals went back to where they came from," decided Miss Nile.

It took us *ages* to catch them all.

Miss Nile put her gold bangle back on and twisted it three times. The animals vanished at once. When we looked at Miss Nile's bangle they were back where they belonged.

Peter climbed down from his table and sank to the floor like a wobbly jelly.

"It wasn't only pets that were mummified,"

said Miss Nile. "The Egyptians thought some animals were earthly versions of the gods. So, when these animals died, they were gift-wrapped as presents for the gods."

"You mean they didn't just mummify cats?" said Jane.

"Oh, no," said Miss Nile. "Baboons, crocodiles, birds, fish… You can see a tomb full of mummified sacred bulls in Egypt. In fact, the ancient Egyptians would mummify almost anything that moved!"

"Better keep still Sammy," whispered Sean to me.

"Did they take out the animal's liver and brain and everything?" asked Sunny, making a face.

"Yes! Mummifying a cat is much the same as mummifying a human," nodded Miss Nile enthusiastically. "They stored all the organs in jars, stuffed the body with sawdust and natron and – hey presto – you'd got a cat ready to wrap."

We all stared at the cat mummy, which was still sitting silently on Miss Nile's desk.

"It looks sort of surprised," I said.

"You'd look surprised if you'd been stuffed with sawdust!" said Sunny.

Kevin put up his hand. He'd been looking baffled for the entire lesson.

"But why steal a *cat*?" he asked. "What's the point?"

It was Miss Nile's turn to look baffled. "Steal? What are you talking about?"

"The tomb robbers!" said Kevin. "I thought you were going to tell us about them."

Miss Nile clapped a hand to her head. "So I was! I got so interested in pet mummies that I completely forgot, Kevin."

"Can't you tell us now?" asked Kevin, disappointed.

"I'll do better than that," said Miss Nile. "I'll ask someone who's a real expert on tomb robbery. But you'll have to wait till tomorrow…"

Her feet were starting to tap dance again.

Tomb robbers

"Ow!" cried the twins at the beginning of the next lesson. "Who did that?"

A shower of earth had just come flying through the window, landing on their heads. This was followed by a round ball of a man with a large, bushy moustache. He clambered into the room, wearing a baggy tweedy suit and with a kit bag and spade slung over one shoulder. It looked to me as if he'd lost half his glasses.

"This is Professor Archibald Rubble, one of the world's leading experts on ancient

Egypt," said Miss Nile. "He knows all about tomb robbers, don't you, Archie?"

"Robbers? Thundering nuisance!" declared the professor. "Imagine what it's like to discover an ancient tomb. You can't! It's beyond words! Then you break in and find that robbers have got there first and stripped the whole blooming place bare!" His eyes twinkled. He seemed rather jolly for a professor of ancient history.

"Was it easy to rob a tomb then?" I asked.

"Easy? I should say not!" said the professor. "I expect you've heard of the Valley of Kings?" We all nodded. "Sixty nobles and Pharaohs were buried there. Sixty! And you know how many of them were robbed?"

"Um ... three?" asked Julie.

"Almost every blooming one!" thundered the professor. "It's very likely that the same workers who built the tombs came back to rob them later!"

"But didn't they know that it was wrong to steal?" asked Tremble.

"Of course! To the ancient Egyptians robbing a tomb was an awful crime. If you robbed a mummy, you were stealing someone's chance of the afterlife."

"Then why did they do it?" I asked.

"Gold! Jewels!" said the professor. "One royal necklace would be worth more than most peasants earned in a lifetime."

"But what if you got caught? It must have been dangerous," said Jane.

The professor produced a sharp stick from his kit bag. "You've seen sausages cooked on sticks?" he asked. We all nodded.

"That's what happened to tomb robbers. They were stuck on a stick and left to fry in the desert."

"Ugh! Gruesome!" said the twins.

"That's why you had to plan your robbery carefully," said the professor, dropping his voice almost to a whisper.

He tapped his nose with one finger. "Let's say I'm a robber, planning to break into a tomb. What will I need?"

"Dynamite!" suggested Kevin.

The professor shook his head. "Nice idea, but it hadn't been invented in ancient Egyptian times."

"You can't do it on your own, can you?" said Sean. "You'll need a gang."

Professor Rubble brought his fist down on the table, making the pens jump in the air. "Precisely! So who's going to join my gang of tomb robbers?"

We all put our hands up – including Miss Nile. This sounded like fun!

The Pickle Hill Gang

← Diggers and tunnellers

Stonemasons to chisel a way in through doors

Boatsman ← (most royal tombs are on the west bank of the nile, so you need a getaway boat.)

Water Carrier →
-it's hot work tunnelling into a tomb!

← **Lookout**

Cat → **burglar**

"What are we going to steal?" I asked.

"Oh, anything that we can sell," said the professor. "Gold, jewels, statues, even a mummy or two."

"A mummy won't be worth much, will it?" said Kevin.

"Ah, don't forget what's wrapped in the bandages," said the professor. "Gold amulets – magic charms to protect the mummy. For robbers, it's like unwrapping a birthday present! Take the tomb of Queen Nefertari. The thieves took everything, even the mummy's bandages. All that was left of her was her knees!"

"I expect they didn't *kneed* them!" said Sunny.

We all groaned. Some of Sunny's jokes should be locked in a tomb.

"But you said not *all* of the tombs were robbed," said Sean.

"That's right, there was one famous tomb that was missed," said Miss Nile, her left foot beginning to drum on the floor.

"Yes, indeed," said Professor Rubble, his eyes shining. "Think of it, the fabulous tomb of a boy Pharaoh hidden for thousands of years. Anyone know his name…?"

"I know! Tutankhamun," said Jane. "He was one of the famous Pharaohs on the coins."

"Why was his tomb never robbed?" asked Julie.

"That's the mystery," said Miss Nile. "Robbers broke in, but they hardly took anything."

"So are we all ready to go?" said the professor, pulling out his spade.

"Go where?" we asked.

"You don't mean we're going to rob it?" gasped Tremble. "Won't that be … dangerous?"

"Did I say rob?" chuckled the professor. "There's no harm in taking a nose around."

He pulled out a gold watch on a chain and checked it. "If we go now, we'll arrive in 1287 BC, just 50 years after Tutankhamun was buried."

Tutankhamun's tomb? I couldn't wait. Maybe we'd bump into some real tomb robbers or, better still, see the royal mummy in its grave!

Raiders of the lost tomb

Professor Rubble shone his torch under our computer desk, then crawled right underneath!

"Well, what are you waiting for?" said Miss Nile. "Let's go!"

One by one we crawled under the desk. Instead of a wall and a plug point, we came to a dark jagged hole, which I'm sure hadn't been there before. I crawled into the hole and found I could almost stand upright. A set of stone steps led down steeply.

"It looks dark down there," shuddered Tremble.

"Nonsense!" The professor's voice echoed up from down below. "Keep close together and follow me."

We went down the rough stone staircase, almost bumping our heads on the low roof.

"Where are we?" I whispered to Miss Nile.

"Under the Valley of Kings," she replied. "Most tombs had a hidden staircase like this one that led down under the rock."

It was very cool in the passageway and our voices echoed even when we whispered. The thought that real tomb robbers had been this way made the hair prickle on the back of my neck. The passage led down and down until we reached an ancient stone door. Professor Rubble shone his torch on a small hole at one corner of the door.

"That's where the robbers must have tunnelled through," said Miss Nile excitedly. "Just think, on the other side of this door, all the treasures of Tutankhamun are waiting."

"Er … there won't be guards or anything?" I asked nervously.

"They'll be guarding the entrance to the tomb above our heads," said the professor cheerfully. "I wouldn't make too much noise, though. We don't want to be caught like the last robbers, do we?"

I certainly didn't want to end up like a sausage on a stick. We did our best to be as quiet as mice as we squeezed through the small hole into the dark chamber beyond. The darkness was so inky that I couldn't see a thing until I shone my torch around. I gasped.

The scene before our eyes was like an Aladdin's cave. Gold and jewels winked back

at us from the shadows. Every corner of the chamber was heaped with statues, boxes, caskets, thrones and beds, all thrown together as if they were worthless.

"Go on, then," Miss Nile said. "Here's your chance to explore a real mummy's tomb. You might be surprised at what you find."

She disappeared into another part of the chamber, leaving us all by ourselves!

We split up to explore. It was like being let loose in a treasure house!

SUNNY TRIED OUT THE PHARAOH'S THRONE FOR SIZE

AHH, THIS IS THE AFTERLIFE!

KEVIN INVESTIGATED THE CANOPIC JARS

UGH! LIVER AGAIN!

JANE TRIED ON SOME OF THE PHARAOH'S WIGS

I'VE ALWAYS WANTED DARK HAIR!

QUEENIE FOUND SOME VERY SMALL SERVANTS

Model servants called Shabti. Meant to work for the Pharaoh in the next world.

Then, all of a sudden, Tremble burst in, shaking like a leaf…

I S-S-SAW HIM!

WHO?

TUTANKHAMUN!

DON'T BE DAFT, TREMBLE. HE'S DEAD!

We'd been so busy exploring the tomb that we'd forgotten all about Tutankhamun's mummy. Tremble pointed towards the burial chamber. "In there," he said. Shining our torches and hardly daring to breathe, we entered the next room. What if Tremble was right and Tutankhamun *was* alive?

"You go first, Sammy," said Sean.

"Thanks a million," I said.

We had to squeeze past an enormous stone box that almost filled the whole room. To our relief we found that Professor Rubble had beaten us to it. He beckoned to us, shining his torch into the enormous box.

We all stared at the shining gold coffin, carved in the shape of the Pharaoh himself.

The painted blue eyes were staring straight at us. No wonder Tremble thought he was being watched!

"You mean that Tutankhamun's actual mummy is in there?" asked Sean in a whisper.

The professor nodded. "Makes you shiver, doesn't it? There are three golden coffins, all as lifelike as that one. The mummy is inside the third one."

Before Professor Rubble could say any more, we heard footsteps from the next chamber. We all froze. The footsteps were coming this way, and getting louder. Had the tomb guards overheard us? If so, we were trapped in the tomb with no way out!

"I don't want to die!" whimpered Tremble.

"We'll be tortured," said the twins.

"Left to fry in the desert!" I moaned.

Sure enough, two tall, bare-chested figures appeared in the entrance to the chamber. There was no mistaking the royal temple guards, armed with spears. And they didn't look as if they'd come to give us a guided tour!

"Um ... isn't there another way out of here?" I asked the professor. "A secret door or something?"

Professor Rubble shook his head. "Sadly not. Looks like we're in a bit of a fix."

"It's OK! We were just going!" smiled Sunny. But when he stepped forward, the guards barred his way and raised their spears threateningly. This time, it looked as if we couldn't escape.

Suddenly, Tremble pointed behind the guards and gasped.

The guards let out a howl of terror, dropped their spears and fled.

We all stood rooted to the spot as the mummy shuffled into the chamber and came to a halt. Slowly it began to unwind the bandages from its head. I could hardly bear to look. I expected to see the mummy's ancient face with the bones showing through the skin. But instead, I saw long black hair and a pair of gold earrings winking back at me.

Miss Nile explained that she'd found the rolls of linen in a box and had been unable to resist playing a trick on us. She said she knew nothing about the guards. It was just lucky for us she came along at the right moment and scared the living daylights out of the ancient Egyptians.

"Miss Nile, you're a marvel!" said Professor Rubble. He twirled his moustache and kissed her hand.

"Time to go, I think," said Miss Nile, turning a shade of pink.

She shone her torch back towards the entrance to the tomb. "Come on, climb through quickly!" she said. "We need to get out of here before those guards come back and realize their mistake."

We clambered through the hole … and found ourselves back in class 5B.

"We never did get to see Tutankhamun's mummy," said Jane. "What happened to it in the end?"

"It was found in 1922 when the tomb was opened," said Miss Nile. "If you visit the Valley of the Kings, you can still see it today."

Right on time, the bell rang and we began to pack up our bags. We all filed out of the classroom, talking excitedly about all the things we'd seen and done this week. Meeting a Pharaoh and breaking into a mummy's tomb! No one would ever believe us. But then, let's face it, every day at Pickle Hill is pretty hard to believe.

Halfway down the corridor, I realized that I'd left my pencil case behind and went back to the classroom. "Great mummy lessons, Miss…" I started to say. But Miss Nile had gone again. Vanished without a trace. There was only a book about ancient Egypt lying open on her desk. I flicked through the pages, until I came to a picture that caught my eye. It was a statue from 1550 BC showing an ancient Egyptian queen. The queen was holding a green-eyed cat on her lap and smiling, but the really weird thing was this – she looked *exactly* like Miss Nile.

But that's just not possible, is it?